C0-GCB-167

Juvenile BV 2793 .H43

Heath, Lou Mishler.

Ed Taylor: father of migrant
missions

LEARNING RESOURCES
CENTER
COLUMBIA BIBLE COLLEGE
P.O. Box 3122
Columbia, SC 29230

# Ed Taylor:
## Father of Migrant Missions

LOU HEATH

Illustrated by Jack Woodson

BROADMAN PRESS
Nashville, Tennessee

To
The boys and girls
at Two Rivers Baptist Church

© Copyright 1982 • Broadman Press
All rights reserved.
ISBN: 0-8054-4278-2
4242-78

Dewey Decimal Classification: J266.092
Subject headings: TAYLOR, ED//MIGRANT LABOR—MISSIONS
Library of Congress Catalog Card Number: 81-70911
Printed in the United States of America

Juvenile
BV
2793
.H43

# Contents

# A Nighttime Horse Ride

Edward quickly saddled the horse. "Hurry, Edward," his father called. "Tell the doctor to come as fast as he can to help your mother!"

The Taylors lived in Greeleyville, South Carolina. The town had no doctor. The Taylors did not have a telephone. Edward must ride the horse five miles to get the doctor.

Nine-year-old Edward had made this trip many times to get medicine or to ask the doctor to come to his home. He wished the moon was a little brighter as he started down the road at a quick trot.

Edward's mother had been sick for as long as Edward could remember. Lots of times he stayed home with his mother while his father worked in the cotton fields or as a house painter.

## Growing Up Years

The Taylors did not have much money, but they loved God. Edward and his younger brother, Jack, went to church. They walked a mile to go to Sunday School.

When Edward was nine years old, his mother talked to him about Jesus' love. She told Edward how to become a Christian. Edward thought about the things his mother said. He asked questions and listened to his mother's answers. Soon he became a Christian. He then joined the church and was baptized.

Each spring, the Taylor family planted a big garden. Edward took extra vegetables to town to sell to help pay bills at home. Edward had saved his money from selling eggs, and fruits and vegetables. When he had enough money, he bought a wagon. He put the vegetables from the garden in the wagon and pulled it on the dirt road to town.

Greeleyville was a friendly town of about five hundred people. There was no daily newspaper in Greeleyville. People got newspapers from the city of Columbia. When Edward was ten years old, he began to deliver newspapers to the people in Greeleyville. When the weather was bad, his father often delivered papers for him.

Edward walked two miles to school. His school had only one room and one teacher. All the children were in the same room no matter what grade they were in.

Edward liked sports but did not play much. He made good grades, but he missed lots of school. Many days he stayed home with his sick mother.

## Going to Work

Edward's full name was John Edward Taylor. As he got older he liked to be called J. Ed or just Ed.

When Ed was fifteen years old, his family moved to Florida. Ed missed school often to stay home and take care of his mother. He finally decided to quit school and get a job. The money he made

working helped pay for food and clothing for the family.

Three years later, Ed and his family moved again. This time, they moved to Columbia, South Carolina. Ed went to work in a cloth-making business. Ed wanted to be a good worker. He ordered lessons about his work through the mail. And he studied at night. He studied and worked hard. Before long, J. Ed was made supervisor at the mill where he worked.

Two important things happened to J. Ed while he worked at the mill. First, he met a girl named Lillie Alberta. Ed liked Alberta, and they became good friends. He told her about Jesus. She too became a Christian. Sometime later Ed and Alberta were married.

Another important thing happened. Ed knew that God wanted him to become a minister. Ed thought he was too old to become a minister. He thought he had not gone to school enough to be a minister.

Ed thought he would help start some churches. He thought God would be happy with him. He started a Wednesday morning prayer service in his aunt's home. Every week for seventeen years, there was a prayer service.

But Edward was not happy. "I knew I was not doing what God wanted me to do," he said. Ed quit his job and moved to Charleston. He got a job there and helped start another church.

## Ed Becomes a Pastor

God still wanted J. Ed Taylor to become a minister. Finally, when he was thirty-six, J. Ed said yes to God. J. Ed, his wife, and their two children moved to Greenville, South Carolina. Ed went to college there as a special student.

After a while, Ed became the pastor of two churches. Soon one church grew so much that J. Ed needed to be there all the time.

J. Ed visited people in their homes. He walked from home to home. Some of the people lived far back in the mountains. He told the people about Jesus. Many of these people became Christians.

J. Ed Taylor was pastor of different churches at different times. At every church he taught the people to love each other and to love missions. Many people learned to know and love Jesus from Ed and Alberta Taylor.

MIGRATORY
WORKERS

## God Does Call Grandparents

Many years passed. Ed Taylor was pastor of a church in Newberry, South Carolina. He was happy to be pastor of that church.

One day, Alberta Taylor taught a group of girls. They studied a story about people who travel from place to place gathering fruits and vegetables. The people are called migrants.

Later she told Ed about their study. "I believe you and I could be happy doing this work," she said.

"What work?" he asked.

"Work with migrants," she told him.

Ed was not very interested. "I do not know anything about that work," he said. "Besides, God does not call grandmothers and grandfathers to be missionaries."

"That may be so," Mrs. Taylor said. "But I told the girls that if God would call us, I would be willing to go."

Ed was surprised. "Well, we will have to pray a lot about that!" he said.

The next week, Ed Taylor read a story about someone who had done wonderful things for migrants. Ed bowed his head and prayed. "Dear God, help me be willing to go anywhere you want me to go."

Ed could hardly wait to tell Alberta. They talked and then they prayed.

Ed called the Home Mission Board. "We feel God wants us to work with migrants," he said. Ed knew that this was what God wanted him and Alberta to do. Every day, he learned, people at the Home Mission Board had prayed for someone to work with migrants.

Soon, Ed and Alberta became migrant missionaries. Ed was forty-seven years old when he and Alberta left their home to begin work that would take them many miles.

BOOKS

## A Home on Wheels

The Taylors now lived in a trailer. When they traveled, they fastened the trailer to their car. And they traveled a lot. They went to twelve different states in their work.

The first place they went was to Oklahoma. There they found three thousand Spanish-speaking migrant workers. The Taylors knew one word in Spanish, *Adios.* The Taylors felt like saying *Adios,* which means good-bye. But they knew God would not want them to give up so easily.

The migrant workers lived in camps. Usually the camps were owned by farmers. Many times the camps were old houses no one lived in. Sometimes they were tin shacks. Many of the houses were not good places for people to live.

The Taylors visited the migrant camps. They tried to show the migrants they wanted to be friends. Ed talked to the camp managers and crew leaders. "We want to show love and care to the people," he said.

Ed tried to find a church or a building where the migrants could have a worship service. One time a chicken house was cleaned and used for a church building.

People from nearby churches often helped the Taylors have Bible schools for the migrant boys and girls. Sometimes they met in church buildings. Sometimes they had Bible school outside under a tree or in a tent. One time they had Bible school in the chicken house.

The boys and girls listened to stories about Jesus. They made things that helped them know about Jesus. The boys and girls often did not have toothbrushes or soap or combs to help them look clean and neat. People in churches in many places sent health kits with such things in them. Mr. and Mrs. Taylor gave the kits to the boys and girls.

One night, Ed asked a friend who spoke Spanish to ride with him in a truck through the camp. He used a loudspeaker to invite the men to hear about Jesus. Some of the men came to the service before they went home to eat supper. A lot of the men accepted Jesus as their Savior. Ed was so excited he could hardly sleep.

Two nights later at another camp, Ed told a large group of men about Jesus. This time more than two hundred men became Christians.

Ed gave the men Spanish New Testaments. But he had only two hundred. The men who did not get the New Testaments were sad. They begged J. Ed to give them a Bible. The next day he found some more New Testaments. But when he took them to the camp, the men had moved to another place.

## A Brace for Henry

One migrant boy Ed and Alberta Taylor met was Henry. Henry was twelve years old. Henry had to stay behind in the camp

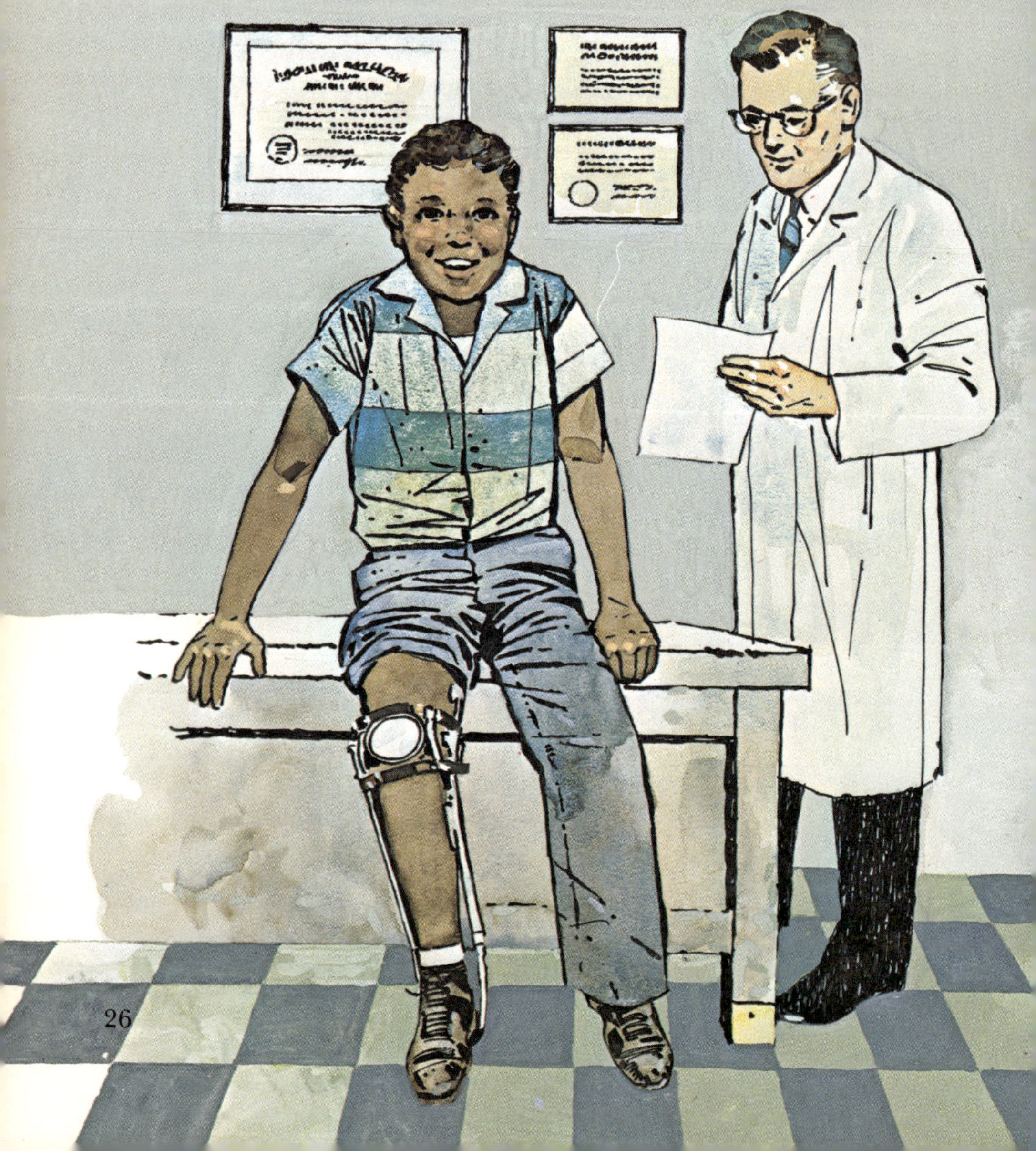

while others in his family went to the fields to work. Henry was crippled. He had to wear a brace on his leg to help him walk. But now his leg was too big for the brace. He needed a new brace. Henry had to lift his leg with his hand when he tried to walk.

Ed decided to help Henry get a new brace. A new brace cost a lot of money, but Ed thought of a way to get the money. He told people in the churches about Henry. One woman gave the money she had saved to fix some furniture. Another woman gave money she and her husband had saved to build a workshop. Both decided Henry needed a new brace more than they needed the things they wanted.

Ed took Henry to the doctor. The doctor examined Henry and ordered a new brace. Ed also told Henry and his parents about Jesus.

## A Comb for Pedro

Pedro came to a service in the chicken house. Pedro was twelve. The first time Pedro came, he kept his cap on all the time.

"Pedro," Mr. Taylor said, "you should take your cap off in the service."

"Señor, me no take off my cap," Pedro said.

"Why?" Mr. Taylor asked.

"My hair not combed," Pedro answered.

"Go ahead and take your cap off, Pedro," Mr. Taylor told him. "After the service, I'll give you a comb."

Mr. Taylor gave Pedro a health kit. It had a comb, a towel, soap, washcloth, a toothbrush, and some toothpaste.

The next night Pedro came in. He looked clean and neat. He came in and sat by Mr. Taylor.

"Me take my cap off tonight," he said. "Me have a comb for it."

SOAP

# Father of Migrant Missions

People in South Carolina say that J. Ed Taylor is the father of migrant missions in their state. For four years, the Taylors worked with migrants in Florida, Georgia, and South Carolina.

Everywhere they went, the Taylors talked to people in the churches. They helped the churches know how to help migrants and tell them about Jesus.

Later J. Ed Taylor went to work at the Home Mission Board. He was in charge of migrant mission work in all the states. He showed churches everywhere how to help the migrants. And he asked more people to be missionaries for migrants.

J. Ed Taylor and Alberta Taylor liked to work with the migrants. And the migrants loved Alberta and J. Ed Taylor. From the Taylors, the migrants learned about Jesus.

## Remember

J. Ed Taylor taught the church people to care for and help the migrants in their area. Sometimes there were no migrants. Then Ed asked the people to give money or supplies for migrants in other places.

Are there migrants in your area? What can you do for them?

Are there new boys and girls in your school? Can you be friendly and kind even if their skin and speech is different from yours?

Ask your pastor or teacher if your church can collect items for a migrant missionary to use.

## About the Author

Lou Heath lives in Nashville, Tennessee. Before Lou and her family moved to Nashville, they lived in different states. Some of the time they lived in places where the migrants worked. Lou thought about migrant friends she knew as she wrote this book.

Lou has written two other books for boys and girls. They are *Daniel: Faithful Captive* and *God Loves Me, Too.*